Cienfu

Art of Cuba

Rebecca Hinson

In loving memory of my mother, Elizabeth Maxine Hinson

Library of Congress Control Number: 2014912789
Edited by Dr. Richard Lederer & John Robuck
History Consultant: Roy Bartolomei
Architecture Consultant: Edward Z. Wronsky, Jr., AIA
Photo on page 18 by Jerome Ryan
Photo on page 23 by Daniel Slavin
Common Core Question Assessments available with bulk purchases.
Rebecca Hinson Publishing
rebeccahinson@rebeccahinsonpublishing.com
www.rebeccahinsonpublishing.com
1-561-267-5756
Lake Worth, Florida
Available in English, hardcover, softcover and digital format.
Printed in the United States of America
ISBN 978-1-938360-36-7

CIENFUEGOS

On the southern central coast of Cuba lies the city of Cienfuegos. The Spanish colonial town was created in the styles of the Romans, the French, and the Moors.

Juan Luis Lorenzo De Clouet founded Fernandina de Jagua in 1819. The first colonists were French. They were soon joined by immigrants from Spain, Venezuela, and the United States.

The town was laid out in a grid of 25 blocks surrounding a large central plaza. As the town grew, more blocks were added.

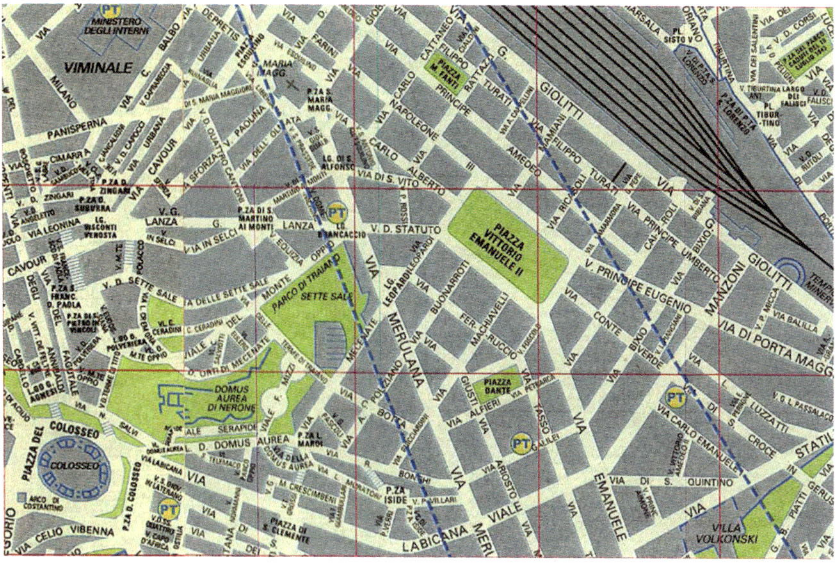

City planning in a grid pattern first began in ancient Rome. The Romans also placed large public buildings in a central plaza.

De Clouet and other colonists purchased field slaves and began planting sugar cane, tobacco, and coffee. After a hurricane destroyed the colony, the colonists rebuilt, renaming the town Cienfuegos.

By the 1830s, Cuba had 1,500 sugar mills for processing sugar and was the world's largest sugar producer and richest colony. Slavery remained the harsh reality for most sugar workers.

Following the classical tradition of ancient Rome, wealthy Cienfuegos planters and traders created grand public buildings on the central plaza of their park.

The Government Palace has a red vaulted dome topped by a cupola.

The cathedral has two large bell towers, three arched entrances, and French stained glass windows.

The former lyceum was designed for elegant dances with orchestral music and casino games.

Allegorical figures of trade, industry, agriculture, science, and the arts flank the Cienfuegos shield on the San Lorenzo School pediment.

Venezuelan Tomas Terry was a trader in sugar and slaves. He built the Tomas Terry Theatre, where world-class actors and singers performed.

The theatre, with its arched colonnade and balconies, was built with Italian marble and hand-carved Cuban hardwoods.

Renowned French actress Sarah Bernhardt thrilled Cienfuegos patrons with her portrayal of Cleopatra.

The interior design of the theatre recalls that of . . .

. . . the Palais Garnier opera house in Paris, France.

The Palacio de Valle has three towers. The Venetian tower on the left symbolizes love. The Moorish tower in the center symbolizes religion. The French tower on the right symbolizes power.

The Palacio de Valle's Moorish style is prominent in Cuba. It was first created by medieval Muslims, who once ruled over what is now Spain, Portugal, and part of France and Italy.

A staircase winds up into the Palacio de Ferrer dome.

The central park was later named after José Martí, the national hero of Cuba. Martí spent his life promoting Cuba's liberty from Spain.

After the Cuban War of Independence, a triumphal arch was built at the entrance of José Martí Park to celebrate Cuba's victory.

Inside the park, a bronze sculpture honors Beny Moré, the great Cuban singer of most genres of Cuban music, the son montuno, mambo, guaracha, and bolero.

Influenced by Roman, French, and Moorish architecture, Cienfuegos is one of Cuba's most beautiful cities.

CPSIA information can be obtained
at www.ICGtesting.com
Printed in the USA
BVIC01n1011191017
497531BV00009B/6
* 9 7 8 1 9 3 8 3 6 0 3 6 7 *